RARE AND PRECIOUS METALS

URANIUM

By Tyrone Mineo

Gareth Stevens
Publishing

Please visit our website, www.garethstevens.com. For a free color catalog of all our high-quality books, call toll free 1-800-542-2595 or fax 1-877-542-2596.

Library of Congress Cataloging-in-Publication Data

Shea, Therese.
Uranium / by Therese Shea.
    p. cm. — (Rare and Precious Metals)
Includes index.
ISBN 978-1-4824-0534-7 (pbk.)
ISBN 978-1-4824-0535-4 (6-pack)
ISBN 978-1-4824-0531-6 (library binding)
1. Uranium — Juvenile literature. I. Shea, Therese. II. Title.
QD137.U73 S54 2014
546.431—dc23

Published in 2014 by
Gareth Stevens Publishing
111 East 14th Street, Suite 349
New York, NY 10003

Designer: Nicholas Domiano
Editor: Therese Shea

Photo credits: Cover, p. 1 Auscape/UIG/Getty Images; pp. 3–24 (inset graphic) Aleksandr Bryliaev/Shutterstock.com; pp. 3–24 (caption box) Hemera/Thinkstock.com; pp. 3–24 (text background) iStockphoto/Thinkstock.com; p. 5 DEA/PHOTO 1/Getty Images; p. 7 (main) Michael Fuller/Flickr/Getty Images; pp. 7 (map), 21 Volina/Shutterstock.com; p. 9 David Boyer/National Geographic/Getty Images; p. 11 Jeff Pachoud/AFP/Getty Images; p. 13 querbeet/E+/Getty images; p. 15 Stan Honda/AFP/Getty Images; p. 17 BIOPHOTO ASSOCIATES/Photo Researchers/Getty Images; p. 19 DEA/De Agostini/Getty Images.

Printed in the United States of America

CPSIA compliance information: Batch #CW14GS: For further information contact Gareth Stevens, New York, New York at 1-800-542-2595.

Contents

Words in the glossary appear in **bold** type the first time they are used in the text.

Power Metal

Have you ever heard of the **element** uranium? It's sometimes talked about in the news. It's an important fuel in some power plants that make electricity.

Uranium is a kind of element called a metal. It's hard and **dense**. It's shiny when rubbed, or polished. Uranium is malleable, which means it can be shaped and bent without breaking. It's ductile, which means it can be stretched into wire. Uranium is also the heaviest element found in nature!

METAL MANIA!

Unlike other metals, uranium doesn't carry, or conduct, electricity very well.

4

The **mineral** uraninite, shown here,
is a major source of uranium.

5

Traces in Many Places

Uranium is found in many kinds of rocks and even in ocean waters! But not enough uranium can be taken from these sources to be useful. The most important sources of uranium include the minerals uraninite, pitchblende, carnotite, and autunite. Because they're sources of metals, these minerals are called ores.

Uranium ore **deposits** can be found both near Earth's surface and very deep under it. People remove ore by digging wide holes called open pits or by digging underground tunnels to reach the deposit.

METAL MANIA!

All the uranium on Earth is the result of a large star exploding more than 5 billion years ago.

top uranium producers

Kazakhstan

Canada

Australia

You can see from this photo of a uranium mine how the term "open-pit mining" got its name. Kazakhstan, Canada, and Australia are the top uranium producers in the world.

Milling Uranium

To produce a useful form of uranium, the uranium ore that's removed from the earth is first milled. That means it's crushed into tiny pieces. It's then mixed with water and **chemicals** to help separate the uranium from other elements in the ore. The form of uranium that results is called yellowcake, but it's not always yellow.

Yellowcake is still not ready to be used as a fuel, though. The process of turning uranium into a form that we can use is called "enrichment."

METAL MANIA!

Yellowcake can be brown or black, rather than yellow. Yellowcake's color depends on the temperature at which it's dried.

Yellowcake is a powdery mixture of uranium and oxygen.

9

Enriching Uranium

There are different types of uranium **atoms** even in the same yellowcake. These are called isotopes. Enriched uranium has a large amount of one kind of isotope. To produce this form of uranium, the yellowcake is changed into a gas. The gas may be passed through a **membrane** until the isotopes are sorted by weight.

Uranium can also be enriched with centrifuges. A centrifuge is a machine that separates atoms by spinning very quickly. After the uranium has been enriched, it's changed into a solid again.

METAL MANIA!

Uranium gas may be passed through a membrane more than a thousand times!

10

It takes a lot of energy to create enriched uranium. The uranium isotope needed for **nuclear** energy makes up less than 1 percent of all uranium!

11

Useful Uranium

Enriched uranium is used to create nuclear power. When an atom of uranium is split in two, it lets out a great amount of heat energy. In a nuclear power plant, this process, called fission (FIH-shun), takes place in a container called a reactor. Fission is carefully controlled in reactors.

The energy from nuclear fission is used to heat water, making steam. The steam spins machines called turbines. This creates electricity that runs through power lines to homes, businesses, and other places.

METAL MANIA!

Enriched uranium is also used to make bombs and other **weapons**.

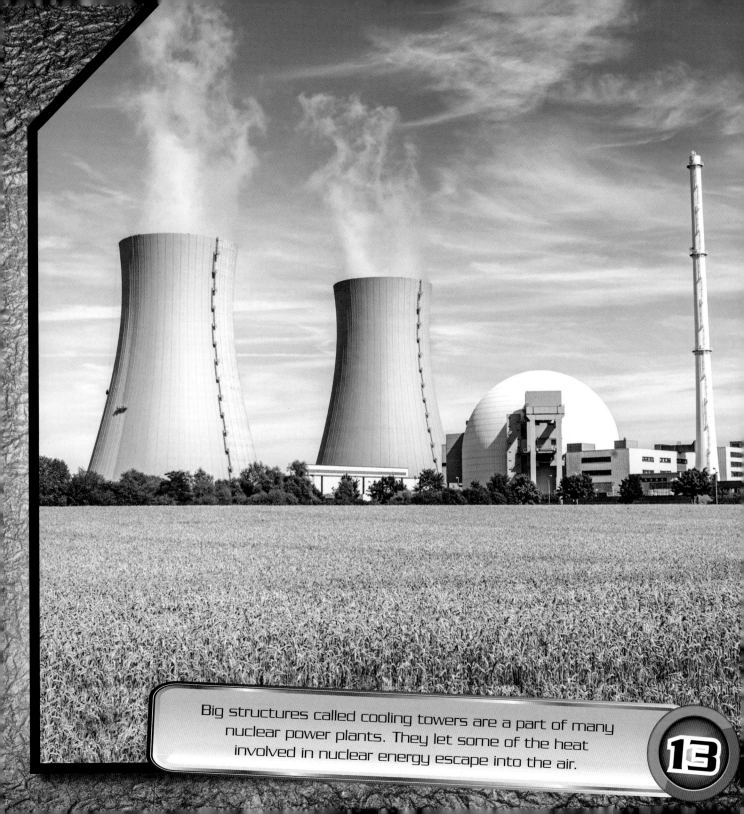

Big structures called cooling towers are a part of many nuclear power plants. They let some of the heat involved in nuclear energy escape into the air.

13

Depleted Uranium

Uranium is very precious because even a small amount can create a huge amount of energy. It's very expensive to make a usable form, so not every country does.

A form of uranium called depleted uranium is a **byproduct** of the long enrichment process. This kind of uranium cannot be used for nuclear power. However, it's still useful because it's very dense and hard. Depleted uranium is used by the military to make shields and weapons. It's also used to make airplanes and ships.

METAL MANIA!

The United States has more than 100 nuclear reactors. About 20 percent of US electricity comes from nuclear power.

Depleted uranium is used to make bullets and **missiles**.

15

Radioactive

Natural uranium is mildly **radioactive**, but enriched uranium is very radioactive. That means it gives off energy called radiation. Everyone is exposed to a small amount of radiation every day. This isn't harmful. However, radiation in large amounts can have terrible, even deadly, effects on the human body.

Enriched uranium must be handled very carefully. It shouldn't be breathed or taken into the body in any way. People who work with radioactive materials wear special suits and masks to avoid harm.

METAL MANIA!

Uranium is very reactive. That means it combines with other elements easily. However, nearly all these mixtures are poisonous!

DANGER
RADIOACTIVE
MATERIAL

About 80 percent of radiation comes from nature. The remaining 20 percent comes from man-made sources.

Discovering Uranium

Even though nuclear power hasn't been around for very long, uranium has been used in other ways throughout history. It was added to glass for many years to give it a yellow or green color. At that time, though, people really didn't know what it was.

In 1789, German scientist Martin Klaproth was studying pitchblende. He realized it contained an undiscovered element. He called the element "uranium" after the planet that had been discovered in 1781—Uranus!

METAL MANIA!

French scientist Eugène Péligot was the first to separate pure uranium from pitchblende in 1841.

Yellow glass containing uranium has to be handled carefully because of uranium's poisonous properties.

19

Cleaner Energy

The use of uranium to make weapons makes many people fear it. They worry that reactors will leak and that radiation will make people deathly ill. However, others believe that it's still a better, cleaner power source than burning **fossil fuels**, such as coal and oil.

Scientists are working hard to make renewable resources, such as water and sunlight, widespread and effective power sources. Until then, nuclear power plants will continue to be built, and uranium will be continue to be an important fuel source.

World Use of Nuclear Power

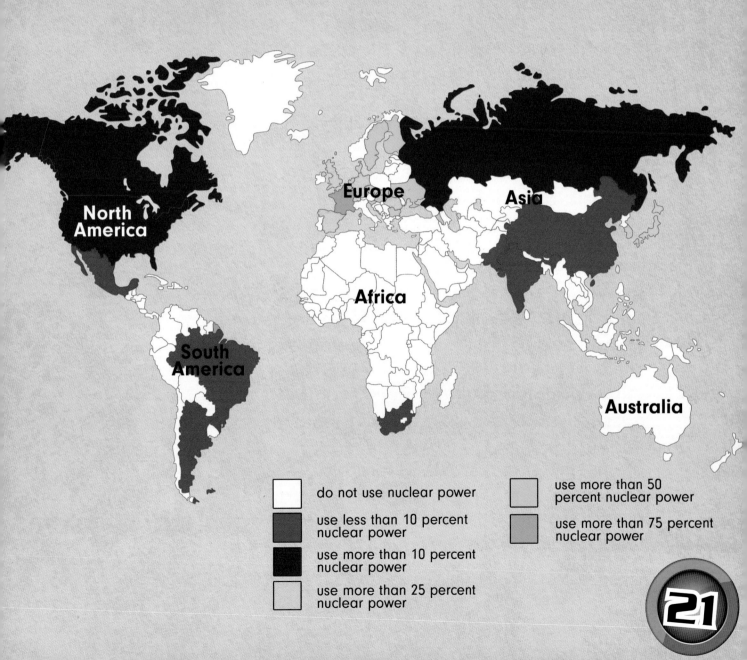

North America

Europe

Asia

South America

Africa

Australia

- do not use nuclear power
- use less than 10 percent nuclear power
- use more than 10 percent nuclear power
- use more than 25 percent nuclear power
- use more than 50 percent nuclear power
- use more than 75 percent nuclear power

21

Glossary

atom: one of the smallest bits of matter

byproduct: something produced as a result of the making of something else

chemical: matter that can be mixed with other matter to cause changes

dense: packed very closely together

deposit: an amount of a mineral in the ground that built up over a period of time

element: matter, such as uranium, that is pure and has no other type of matter in it

fossil fuel: matter formed over millions of years from plant and animal remains that is burned for power

membrane: a soft, thin layer of something that only very small bits of matter can pass through

mineral: matter in the ground that forms rocks

missile: a rocket used to strike something at a distance

nuclear: having to do with the power created by splitting atoms, the smallest bits of matter

radioactive: putting out harmful energy in the form of tiny particles

weapon: something used to cause someone or something injury or death

For More Information

Books

Cooke, Rebecca. *Examining Nuclear Energy*. Minneapolis, MN: Clara House Books, 2013.

Owen, Ruth. *Energy from Atoms: Nuclear Power*. New York, NY: PowerKids Press, 2013.

Websites

Uranium
www.epa.gov/radiation/radionuclides/uranium.html
Find answers to your questions about uranium.

Uranium (U)
www.robinsonlibrary.com/science/chemistry/elements/uranium.htm
Read more about uranium, and see a map showing where it can be found around the globe.

Uranium Element Facts
www.chemicool.com/elements/uranium.html
Learn more about uranium and nuclear power.

Index